THE
Bits of Bri
COOKBOOK

The secret ingredient is always love!

THE

Bits of Bri

COOKBOOK

BRIANNA SAVOCA KOEHLER

Dedication

To my mom – an incredible cook and homemaker, who made sure we passed down our family recipes. So thankful I got to learn from the best. Love you!

Contents

About Bri

Brianna is a YouTube personality sharing her life and love for homemaking across her social media. She lives in Ohio with her husband and two children, with their third baby due in November 2020.

Cooking is one of the greatest gifts you can give to those you love.

– Ina Garten

Hey Loves!

Welcome to my cookbook!

I remember my mom making countless family dinners when I was a little girl, and our entire house would smell amazing. My gramma also made so many Sunday dinners and special holiday meals over the years, with the entire family gathered around the table to break bread together. My dad would always talk enthusiastically about the special meals his mom made.

There's something about those mom-made meals because they're more than just good food, they're truly made with love.

After having a family of my own, I started sharing life and homemaking videos on my YouTube channel. I would share every day dinners or what I was making for holidays, and my sweet subscribers would always ask for the recipes. So it just made sense to organize all my favorite recipes for you in one place- so this cookbook was born!

It meant so much to gather all my family recipes from both my mom's side and my dad's side, and include the meals certain people loved or made for certain holidays. Just like all these recipes, this cookbook is truly made with love.

xoxo
Brianna K

STARTERS

There's something so fun about appetizers - maybe it's because they're generally shared at parties or girls' nights. They're shared between friends and family for exciting events. They're easy to make.

Same thing with side dishes - they're no frills, but the perfect compliment to the main dish.

For every recipe in this starters section, I have to restrain myself from gobbling up the entire dip, and when it comes to the breads and rolls in this section, I sometimes don't even get a piece because Adam, Landon, and Presley inhale it so fast!

One time after I made the Italian rolls, my mother-in-law stopped by to drop off something. While we were chatting, the kids ate the entire tray of rolls that were sitting on the counter before we even sat down to dinner. I get asked all the time to share these recipes whenever I bring them to a party.

So here's to food and to fun- enjoy!

STARTERS

Lolo's Bacon Cheddar Dip

PREP TIME	REFRIGERATION TIME	SERVINGS
30 mins	60 mins	12+

INGREDIENTS

- 8 oz cream cheese, softened
- 8 oz sour cream
- 1 bunch of green onions, thinly sliced
- 4 medium tomatoes, chopped
- 16 oz salsa

- 2 cups shredded cheese
- 1 pound regular sliced bacon, cooked and crumbled
- 1 large bag of tortilla chips

INSTRUCTIONS

1. In a mixing bowl, add your cream cheese and sour cream and beat until smooth.
2. Spread above mixture on a 12" serving plate in an even layer.
3. Spread your salsa in an even layer on top of the cream cheese and sour cream mixturE.
4. Sprinkle the chopped tomatoes and thinly sliced green onions on top.
5. Cover generously with shredded cheese.
6. Sprinkle the cooked bacon crumble on top as the finishing top.
7. Refrigerate for at least 1 hour, or until ready to serve.

> When I was growing up, my parents always hosted a 4th of July party for our family. Everyone would come over for a bbq, and we'd have a water balloon toss and a slip-and-slide in the backyard. My mom, now called "LoLo" by my kids, would make this dip. If you didn't come on time to party, it would be gone. So some years she started making two platters of this recipe. It is that good!

Grampy's Fried Zucchini

PREP TIME	COOK TIME	SERVINGS
5 mins	10 mins	4-6

INGREDIENTS

- Olive oil or vegetable oil
- 1 - 2 zucchini's
- 3 eggs

- 1 ½ cup Italian bread crumbs
- Salt + pepper

INSTRUCTIONS

1. Cover ¼ inch large frying pan with olive oil and turn element on to medium high heat.
2. In a bowl, whisk eggs and set aside.
3. Cut zucchinis lengthwise into ½" sticks. You can cut the sticks in half if you wish.

4. Dip zucchini in egg, remove and cover each side with salt and pepper, then bread crumbs.
5. Put battered zucchini sticks in the heated oil and fry until golden brown on each side.
6. When ready, carefully remove from frying pan and set on paper towel to drain.

> My grampa is incredible at growing fruits and veggies in his backyard garden. He always has a TON of zucchini. No one can fry it up quite like he can- and this recipe is straight from him!

Buffalo Chicken Dip

PREP TIME	COOK TIME	SERVINGS
5 mins	60 mins	12+

INGREDIENTS

- 1 lb cooked and shredded chicken breast
- 2 (8 oz) packages cream cheese, softened
- 1 cup ranch dressing

- 1 cup buffalo sauce (I like Frank's Red Hot®)
- 2 cups shredded mozzarella cheese (reserve ½ cup)

INSTRUCTIONS

1. Add shredded cooked chicken, cream cheese, ranch dressing, buffalo sauce and 1 ½ cups shredded mozzarella cheese into crockpot and mix well.
2. Cook on high until warmed (approximately 1 hour).
3. Stir and mix ingredients well.

4. Sprinkle reserved ½ cup of cheese on top of each serving.
5. Serve with tortilla chips, celery sticks, carrot chips, or other veggies or chips to dip.

Landon's Favorite Olive Oil Bread

PREP TIME	COOK TIME	SERVINGS
5 mins	25 mins	6 - 8

INGREDIENTS

BREAD:
- 1 roll of French Bread Dough
- Olive oil
- Salt + pepper
- Italian seasoning

DIP:
- Olive oil
- Salt + pepper
- Balsamic vinegar

INSTRUCTIONS

1. Unroll bread dough onto greased baking pan.
2. With a knife, cut diagonal slices half way into the height of the dough.
3. Brush olive oil over the top of the dough.
4. Sprinkle with salt, pepper, and Italian seasoning.
5. Bake in the oven for 25 minutes at 350°F.
6. On a small plate, pour olive oil, a drizzle of balsamic vinegar, salt and pepper.
7. Serve bread warm and dip into olive oil mixture.

> Landon started kindergarten this year, and his teacher had the kids fill out an "All About Me" form. He had to draw a picture of his favorite food- and he drew olive oil bread! He loves it- and we've never had any leftovers when I make a loaf!

Black Bean + Corn Dip

PREP TIME	COOK TIME	SERVINGS
10 mins	0 mins	12+

INGREDIENTS

- 1 (15 oz) can corn
- 1 (15 oz) can black beans
- 1 small red onion
- 2 tbsp chopped garlic

- 1 lime
- 1 bunch cilantro
- Salt + pepper
- Tortilla chips

INSTRUCTIONS

1. Finely chop the red onion, garlic and cilantro and set each aside separately.

2. Mix chopped onion with a drained can of corn, drained can of black beans, chopped garlic and the juice of the lime.

3. Add chopped cilantro and salt and pepper to taste.
TIP: *If there's any leftover (which is rare), I love adding this salsa to my chili recipe!*

Cucumber Salad

PREP TIME	REFRIGERATION TIME	SERVINGS
5 mins	60+ mins	6 - 8

INGREDIENTS

- 2 cucumbers, skinned and thinly sliced
- 1 ½ tsp salt
- 1 ½ tsp sugar
- ½ red onion, thinly sliced
- 3 tbsp red wine vinegar

INSTRUCTIONS

1. In a medium sized mixing bowl, add sliced cucumbers and sprinkle with salt and sugar.
2. Add sliced red onion and vinegar to the bowl.
3. Mix all ingredients together.
4. Refrigerate at least 60 minutes or until serving time.

This recipe is simple, but it is so refreshing! Presley loves this recipe too—sometimes she'll reach right into the bowl even before I serve it, snatching up the cucumbers.

Italian Crescents

PREP TIME	COOK TIME	SERVINGS
10 mins	20 mins	8

INGREDIENTS

- 1 can (8 oz) of crescent roll dough
- 1 cup of shredded mozzarella cheese
- Olive oil
- Italian dressing
- Garlic salt

INSTRUCTIONS

1. Heat oven to 350°F.
2. Remove dough from can, roll it out and separate into 8 triangles (these are precut in the dough).
3. Sprinkle shredded cheese on each dough triangle
4. Roll up each crescent, ending at tip of triangle. Place with tips down in crescent shape.
5. Brush the tops with olive oil.
6. Sprinkle with Italian seasoning and garlic salt.
7. Place on ungreased baking sheet and bake according to package instructions.
8. Serve warm.

Fourth of July Fruit Salad

PREP TIME	REFRIGERATION TIME	SERVINGS
20 mins	1 hour	10 - 15

INGREDIENTS

- 2 cups cubed watermelon
- 1 cup sliced strawberries
- 1 cup blueberries
- 1 cup blackberries
- Jicama

INSTRUCTIONS

1. In a large bowl, mix all fruit together, reserving the jicama.
2. Slice the jicama into 1/4 inch thick slices.
3. Use a small star cookie cutter to make 4-6 jicama stars.
4. Place the stars on the top of the salad.
5. Refrigerate at least 1 hour, until serving time.

Cranberry Brie Cups

PREP TIME	COOK TIME	SERVINGS
10 mins	15 mins	12

INGREDIENTS

- 1 can (8 oz) crescent roll dough
- 1 (8 oz) block brie cheese
- 1 small (14 oz) can cranberry sauce
- 4 sprigs of rosemary

INSTRUCTIONS

1. Preheat oven to 350°F and grease muffin pan.
2. Roll out package of crescent dough.
3. Cut dough into 12 equal square pieces, roughly 2 inches wide.
4. Put one piece of cut dough into each cup of the greased muffin pan.
5. Add one spoonful of cranberry sauce to each piece of crescent dough.
6. Cut block of brie cheese into 12 equal slices.
7. Put one piece of brie into each piece of crescent dough.
8. Fold edges of crescent dough over the cheese and cranberry filling.
9. Bake for 10-15 minutes or until crescent dough is lightly browned.
10. Remove from muffin pan and put on serving plate.
11. Top each cup with a 1 inch sprig of rosemary before serving. Serve warm.

DINNERS

Family Dinners - I loved the feeling of sitting down with my mom, dad, and sister Kali and sharing about our day over one of the delicious meals my mom would make for us.

I still remember the plates - they were cream with tiny pink hearts and blue dotted trim. I remember the sounds of utensils scratching, my dad's warm voice, my mom's laugh, and my sister never wanting to eat her peas.

When I was home from school, I remember my mom starting to cook early in the afternoon. The smells of onion and garlic permeating the kitchen, making me hungry until it was finally suppertime. Especially if she was making city chicken- my favorite mom-made dinner ever!

Some of the last conversations I had with my dad were about those family dinners, and the memories he had of his favorite dinners that his mom made- like her pork, sauerkraut, and dumplings. So here are all our family favorites- the meals made for generations that are truly made with love.

DINNERS

Mom's City Chicken

PREP TIME	COOK TIME	SERVINGS
30 mins	2 hours	8

INGREDIENTS

- 1 egg
- 1 cup flour
- 1 cup bread crumbs
- 1 lb cubed pork (aka "city chicken")
- Salt + pepper
- 4 inch wooden skewers

- Olive oil
- 2 tbsp butter
- 1 cup chicken broth
- 1 (10 oz) can cream of mushroom soup

INSTRUCTIONS

1. Mix up egg in a bowl with ½ cup water.
2. Put flour on one plate.
3. Put bread crumbs on another plate.
4. Wash off pieces of pork under cold water.
5. Dip them in flour to coat them well.
6. Then dip into the egg wash.
7. Salt and pepper the pieces then dip into bread crumbs.
8. Set aside on a plate until all pieces are coated, then add to skewers (about 3 pieces per skewer).
9. Use a deep frying pan with a lid.
10. Heat up ½ inch of olive oil in pan with 2 tbsp of butter melted in it. Turn down to medium heat.
11. Brown pieces of breaded city chicken.
12. Once all pieces are browned, add all skewers back to frying pan and add chicken broth. Cover with lid and turn heat down to low. Let simmer 1.5 to 2 hours.
13. After it's done cooking, remove all meat from pan. If needed, add water until you have about 1 cup liquid in pan. Then add cream of mushroom soup. Bring to a boil and whisk together well to make your gravy. Turn off heat. Serve city chicken hot with mashed potatoes and gravy.

> This recipe is very near and dear to my heart– it is my favorite meal my mom makes. I know it says "chicken," but it is a recipe from the Depression– the story goes that country folk thought wealthy people in the cities made their chicken like this, but pork cost less. So it goes by the name "City Chicken," and it sure is good!

Savoca Sauce + Meatballs

PREP TIME	COOK TIME	SERVINGS
30 mins	3 hours	12

INGREDIENTS

MEATBALLS
- 1 lb ground beef
- 1 sweet onion, finely chopped
- 2 cloves garlic, minced
- 1 cup seasoned bread crumbs
- 1 tsp dried mustard
- 1 tbsp Worcestershire sauce
- 3 tbsp parsley
- 1 egg
- 3 tbsp minced basil (or dried)
- Salt + pepper
- Garlic salt
- 2 tbsp milk

SAUCE
- 2 tbsp chopped garlic, browned in olive oil
- 3 (28 oz) cans tomato sauce
- 1 (28 oz) can diced tomatoes
- 1 small (6 oz) can tomato paste
- 1 tsp garlic salt
- 2 tsp Italian seasoning
- 1 tbsp fresh parsley
- 1 tbsp fresh basil
- 1 cup red wine
- 1 lb thinly sliced boneless pork loin (optional)
- 1 cup parmesan cheese

INSTRUCTIONS

1. Mix meatball ingredients together well. Form into 1 inch balls.
2. Put 2 tbsp chopped garlic in olive oil in large cooking pot on medium heat. Add in meatballs. Cook until lightly browned.
3. Cover meatballs and browned garlic in 3 cans of tomato sauce. Turn to low heat.
4. To sauce, add: paste, garlic salt, pepper, diced tomatoes, Italian seasoning, fresh parsley, basil, and wine.

OPTIONAL: *add in 1 inch slices of pork to flavor sauce*
5. Let sauce simmer on low for at least 3 hours, stirring gently (don't break up the meat balls) every 15-20 minutes to keep bottom of sauce from burning
6. Add 1 cup parmesan cheese 30 minutes before serving to thicken sauce.
7. Serve over pasta. Mangia!

Chicken Alfredo Lasagna

PREP TIME	COOK TIME	SERVINGS
30 mins	1 hour 3 mins	12

INGREDIENTS

- 1 lb ground chicken breast
- 2 tbsp chopped garlic
- 1 (10 oz) package frozen spinach
- 3 (16 oz) jars alfredo sauce
- 1 (15 oz) container ricotta cheese
- ½ cup parmesan cheese
- 1 tbsp Italian seasoning
- 1 box lasagna noodles (oven ready)
- 1 (16 oz) bag shredded mozzarella cheese

INSTRUCTIONS

1. Brown 1 lb ground chicken with two tablespoons of chopped garlic.
2. Add in 1 package of frozen spinach.
3. Pour in 3 jars of Alfredo sauce.
4. Cook on medium heat on the stove, stirring frequently, until sauce is bubbling.
5. In a separate bowl, mix 1 container of ricotta cheese with parmesan cheese and Italian seasoning.
6. Spread layer of chicken alfredo sauce in greased 9×13 pan.
7. Layer noodles, then ricotta mixture, then sauce, then ¼ of the bag of mozzarella cheese three times.
8. Top final layer with an extra layer of cheese.
9. Cover with foil and bake at 350°F for 45 minutes.
10. Remove foil and bake another 15 minutes.
11. Broil for 3 minutes.
12. Let it set for 20-30 minutes before serving.

This is my favorite recipe in the entire cookbook. I've started making it as a part of our Easter dinner, and I look for an excuse to make it any other time of the year too!

Chicken Parmesan

PREP TIME	COOK TIME	SERVINGS
10 mins	20 mins	8

INGREDIENTS

- 2 lbs thinly sliced chicken breast (~8 pieces)
- 2 cups flour
- 2 cups Italian breadcrumbs
- 2 eggs
- ½ cup milk

- 1 cup olive oil
- 1 (16 oz) jar tomato sauce
- 1 cup freshly grated parmesan cheese
- 1 cup shredded mozzarella cheese
- Fresh basil, chopped

INSTRUCTIONS

1. Put 2 cups of flour on one plate and season with salt and pepper.
2. Put 2 cups Italian breadcrumbs on another plate.
3. Whisk together eggs and milk.
4. Wash chicken breasts in water.
5. Dredge in flour, then dip in egg mixture, then dredge chicken breast in breadcrumbs.
6. On medium, heat olive oil in sauté pan. Cook chicken until golden brown on both sides (about 2-3 minutes per side).
7. Add browned chicken to a greased baking dish. Top with a spoonful of tomato sauce (don't add too much or it will make your chicken breading soggy), then sprinkle chicken with cheeses.
8. Bake in oven at 400°F for 5-7 minutes until cheese is bubbly.
TIP: *I like to put mine on broil for 1-2 minutes to make the cheese a tiny bit browned.*
9. Heat remaining pasta sauce on stove and serve with your favorite pasta. Garnish with fresh chopped basil

At-Home Gordita Crunch

PREP TIME	COOK TIME	SERVINGS
10 mins	20 mins	6 - 8

INGREDIENTS

- 1 lb ground beef
- 1 package taco seasoning
- Soft taco tortillas
- Hard taco shells (highly recommend the bold nacho cheese shells)

- 2 cups shredded taco cheese
- Chipotle ranch dressing
- Taco toppings of your choice

INSTRUCTIONS

1. Cook ground beef according to taco seasoning instructions.

2. On baking sheet, lay soft tortillas flat and sprinkle with shredded taco cheese. Bake at 350°F until cheese is melted and bubbly (about 3 minutes).

3. Remove from oven and quickly press the cheese side of the tortilla around the hard taco shells, so it will stick and dry around the hard shell.

4. Fill hard shells with taco meat.

5. Sprinkle with taco cheese and drizzle with chipotle ranch dressing.

6. Add taco toppings of your choice

TIP: *I serve ours with sour cream, sliced jalapeños, black olives, green onions, and salsa.*

Bacon Ranch Cheeseburgers

PREP TIME	COOK TIME	SERVINGS
5 mins	10 – 15 mins	4

INGREDIENTS

- 1 lb ground beef
- ½ package ranch dressing seasoning
- 4 slices cooked bacon
- 4 burger buns

- 4 slices of cheese
- Ranch dressing
- Burger toppings and condiments of your choice

INSTRUCTIONS

1. Mix ranch seasoning with ground beef. Divide into four equal sized patties.

2. Cook on grill or in pan until desired doneness.

3. Toast buns on grill or in oven (350°F for 2-3 minutes).

4. Top burgers with cheese slices last 1-2 minutes of cooking so cheese is melted.

5. Add a slice of bacon, cut into two pieces, on top of each burger.

6. Add burgers to buns and drizzle with ranch dressing.

7. Add desired burger toppings and condiments

TIP: *I serve ours with lettuce, tomatoes, sliced red onion, ketchup, mustard when we have guests.*

Adam's Favorite Pasta

PREP TIME	COOK TIME	SERVINGS
5 mins	25 mins	8

INGREDIENTS

- 1 box fettucini
- 1 (10 oz) package frozen peas - cooked
- 1 lb bacon, cooked and crumbled
- ½ red onion, finely chopped
- 2 tbsp olive oil

- 3 tbsp chopped garlic
- 3 (16 oz) jars alfredo sauce
- 2 cups shredded mozzarella cheese
- Fresh basil, chopped

INSTRUCTIONS

1. In a sauce pan, cook garlic and onions in olive oil on medium heat until onions are soft.
2. Add in 3 jars of Alfredo sauce.
3. Once sauce is bubbling, turn down heat to low and cover. Stir frequently so sauce does not burn.
4. Cook fettucini and peas per package directions separately.
5. Fry bacon until browned, and crumble.
6. Add cooked pasta to large dish or bowl.
7. Pour sauce over pasta, then top with peas and crumbled bacon.
8. Top with the shredded mozzarella cheese.
9. Serve warm. Garnish with fresh chopped basil.

"

Adam loves this pasta! Ever since we've been together, I always make this for special occasions. It has become a staple for our Christmas Eve dinner, when we have an Italian feast.

Best Ever Lasagna

PREP TIME	BAKE TIME	SERVINGS
3 hours 10 mins	1 hour 20 mins	12

INGREDIENTS

MEAT SAUCE

- 3 tbsp olive oil
- 1 red onion, diced
- 2 tbsp minced garlic
- 1 lb ground beef
- 1 lb ground veal
- 2 (24 oz) jars garden style tomato pasta sauce
- 1 tsp Italian Seasoning
- ¼ cup red wine
- Salt to taste

CHEESE LAYER

- 2 cups shredded mozzarella cheese
- ½ cup grated parmesan cheese
- 2 cups whole milk ricotta cheese
- 1 teaspoon Italian seasoning

LAYERING

- 1 pound box oven-ready lasagna noodles
- 2 cups shredded mozzarella cheese

INSTRUCTIONS

1. For the meat sauce, heat olive oil over medium heat in a large pot.

2. Add in onion and garlic and sauté 2 minutes

3. Add in ground beef and veal. Break meat apart until browned completely. Once meat has browned, pour in tomato sauce, Italian seasoning, wine, and salt. Bring to boil, then reduce heat to simmer.

4. Cook sauce 3 hours on low, stirring occasionally, until very thick.

5. While meat sauce cooks, make the cheese layer. Stir cheeses together in a bowl with Italian seasoning, salt & pepper. Set aside.

6. To assemble Lasagna, spread ½ cup prepared sauce in the bottom of a lightly greased 9×13 baking dish. Layer in 5-6 cooked noodles, then spread half of the cheese mixture on top of the noodles. Then one third of the remaining sauce.

Top with more noodles, the second half of the cheese mixture and another third of the sauce. Final layer is the last of the noodles and the last ⅓ of the meat sauce. Sprinkle with the 2 cups shredded mozzarella cheese.

7. To bake: preheat oven to 350°F.

8. Cover lasagna with greased foil. Bake 60 minutes with foil on. Remove foil and bake another 15 minutes or until cheese has browned.

TIP: I usually broil for 3-5 minutes at the end to get the cheese nice, brown, and bubbly!

9. Remove from oven, cover lightly with foil and let lasagna set for 30 minutes before cutting and serving. Sprinkle with dried parsley flakes, cut into squares and serve.

Insta-Pot Roast

PREP TIME	COOK TIME	SERVINGS
15 mins	70 mins	8-10

INGREDIENTS

- 3 lb chuck roast
- Salt + pepper
- 3 tbsp olive oil
- 1 yellow onion, chopped
- 2 tbsp minced garlic
- 1 small (6 oz) can tomato paste
- ¼ cup red wine (I use Apothic Red, still not sponsored)

- 3 cups beef stock
- 1 tbsp Worcestershire sauce
- 4 sprigs fresh thyme
- 1 ½ lbs baby potatoes
- 1 lb package baby carrots
- ⅓ cup of flour
- 2 tablespoons cornstarch

INSTRUCTIONS

1. Set pressure cooker to the high sauté setting.
2. Season beef with salt and pepper. Heat oil in Instant Pot. Add seasoned beef and cook until evenly browned, about 2-3 minutes per side, and set beef aside.
3. Add chopped onion, and cook until soft, about 2-3 minutes, stirring frequently to not burn at the bottom of the pot. Stir in minced garlic and tomato paste, and cook for about 1 minute, still stirring frequently.
4. Stir in red wine, scraping any bits from the bottom of the Instant Pot. Stir in beef stock, Worcestershire, and thyme.

5. Add in potatoes and carrots. Top with beef. Select pressure cook setting and cook on high for 60 minutes.
6. Remove beef, potatoes and carrots from the Instant Pot, and shred beef using two forks.
7. Select high sauté setting. Bring to a boil; stir in flour and cornstarch and cook, stirring frequently, until slightly thickened, about 2-3 minutes. If the mixture is too thick, add more beef stock as needed until desired consistency is reached.
TIP: *I like my gravy thicker- how my mom always made it!*
8. Serve beef, potatoes and carrots with gravy.

Mediterranean Chicken

PREP TIME
10 mins

COOK TIME
4 hours

SERVINGS
4

INGREDIENTS

- 4 boneless skinless chicken breasts
- 1 Italian dressing seasoning packet
- 1 lemon, squeezed
- 2 tbsp garlic, chopped

- 1/2 red onion, chopped
- 1 cup kalamata olives
- 1 cup roasted red peppers
- 2 tbsp capers

INSTRUCTIONS

1. Add chicken to slow cooker.
2. Add onions, olives, red peppers, and capers to slow cooker.

3. Whisk together Italian dressing packet, lemon juice, and garlic and pour over chicken.
4. Cover and cook on low for 4 hours.

Sliders

PREP TIME	COOK TIME	SERVINGS
10 mins	25 mins	12

INGREDIENTS

- 1 lb ground beef
- Salt +pepper
- 1 tbsp minced onion
- 6 slices American cheese
- 1 cup shredded lettuce
- 12 count Hawaiian roll slider buns

- 2 tbsp olive oil
- 1 tbsp sesame seeds
- Thousand Island dressing
- OPTIONAL: 2 tbsp chopped onion
- OPTIONAL: sliced dill pickles

INSTRUCTIONS

1. Preheat oven to 350°F.

2. In a large bowl mix together your ground beef, salt, pepper and minced onion.

3. In a large baking dish (I use a 13x9) press your ground beef into a rectangle.

4. Bake in oven for about 20-25 minutes until internal temp reaches 165°F.

5. Remove dish from oven and top with cheese slices. Place back in oven and bake until cheese is melted.

6. Slice Hawaiian rolls in half.

OPTIONAL: *If you like your buns toasted, place them in oven on separate baking dish for 1-2 minutes (I always toast ours).*

7. Add bottom of slider buns to a separate baking dish, spread thousand island dressing over the bottom of buns, next top with shredded lettuce, then with your ground beef slice.

OPTIONAL: *Sprinkle on your chopped onions and then layer your pickles over top (we skip this step in our house).*

8. Drizzle with Thousand Island dressing. Top with Hawaiian roll slider bun tops.

9. Brush tops with olive oil and sprinkle with sesame seeds

TIP: *If you're toasting your buns, I add the sesame seeds before toasting*

Poppy's Stuffed Peppers

PREP TIME	COOK TIME	SERVINGS
20 mins	60 mins	6

INGREDIENTS

- 6 large bell peppers (any color- flat bottoms)
- 1 lb ground beef
- ½ red onion, finely chopped
- 1 cup cooked rice
- 1 ½ tsp salt
- 1 tsp pepper
- 1 tbsp chopped garlic
- 2 cans (28 oz) diced tomatoes
- Salt + pepper

INSTRUCTIONS

1. Slice the tops of bell peppers off; remove ribs and seeds and set aside.
2. In a skillet over medium heat, cook beef, onions, garlic, salt and pepper for 8 - 10 minutes, stirring frequently, until beef is browned and onions are soft. Drain fat.
4. Stir cooked rice into beef mixture in skillet.
5. Stuff peppers with beef mixture; arrange in large cooking pot.
6. Pour can of diced tomatoes over peppers. Bring tomato sauce to a simmer on medium heat, then turn to low heat. Cover pot with lid, and cook for 1 hour, or until peppers are soft.
7. Use slotted spoon to lift peppers from pot. Serve with mashed potatoes topped with tomato sauce
TIP: *Select bell peppers with flat bottoms, not pointed bottoms, so that they stand up nicely in the pot.*

> *I will never forget the day my mom dropped me off at my Poppy's house in Cleveland, and the smell of the stuffed peppers he was making on the stove. I can never make this recipe without thinking of him.*

GG's Dumplings

PREP TIME	COOK TIME	SERVINGS
60 mins	15 mins	12

INGREDIENTS

- 5 lbs restaurant potatoes
- 1 ¼ cups flour
- 3 eggs

- 1 heaping tbsp salt
- ½ tsp pepper
- 1 sweet red onion, grated

INSTRUCTIONS

1. Peel potatoes.
2. Chop potatoes into pieces and use a blender to grate, a few potatoes at a time, until you have 3 quarts of potato pulp.
3. Use a freshly cleaned pillowcase.
TIP FROM GG: I recommend using a lint roller inside and out), and pour grated pulp inside. Twist pillowcase so potato pulp rests at the bottom. Squeeze water out of potatoes with your hand to remove as much water as possible.
4. Place pulp in large bowl.
5. Add egg, salt, pepper, and grated onion and mix well.

6. Add flour and mix well.
7. In large pot, bring 5 quarts of salted water to a boil.
8. With large serving spoon, form potato mixture into large balls. Lower heat to medium high, and drop balls into water.
9. Cover pot and cook for 20 minutes. Dumplings will rise to top of water when done. Remove with a slotted spoon.
10. Put cooked dumplings into baking dish and drizzle with butter.
11. Can serve immediately, or best if refridgerated overnight and reheated in oven at 300°F for 20 minutes.
TIP FROM GG: Serve with pork roast and gravy

My dad would always talk about his mom's dumplings and my Gramma's dumplings. They were his favorite meal of the year- as we'd eat pork, sauerkraut and dumplings every New Year's Day. This is GG's recipe, and she has a special pillowcase reserved for her dumplings!

FALL

Fall is my favorite season. I think it's always been that way – especially since I loved going back to school.

Growing up in Ohio, we are lucky to have four seasons and gorgeous fall foliage. I love fall decor, fall candles, and fall cooking! So this section is dedicated to some of my favorite hearty fall recipes – perfect for enjoying during football games or after school dinners.

I've also included some delicious fall baking recipes for you to enjoy. When I started dating Adam, I quickly learned he rarely misses a football game for anything, so many of these recipes are ones I like to throw in the crockpot so we can fill our bowls while enjoying a game together as a family.

One of my favorite memories was when Adam let Landon skip his nap to watch an Ohio State Buckeyes game, and Landon was jumping up and down on the couch screaming "O-H" and cheering so loud that he woke up Presley from her nap, so all of us ended up watching the game together.

So put on a cozy sweater, cuddle up on the couch, and enjoy our favorite fall recipes!

FALL

Rainbow Chili

PREP TIME	COOK TIME	SERVINGS
15 mins	4 - 6 hours	8

INGREDIENTS

- 1 lb ground turkey/beef
- 1 can diced tomatoes
- 1 can chili beans
- 1 cup sliced carrots
- 1 can corn

- ½ red onion, chopped
- 1 packet chili seasoning
- 2 tbsp chopped garlic
- Toppings: sliced green onion, sliced jalapenos, sour cream, shredded taco cheese, tortilla chips

INSTRUCTIONS

1. In slow cooker, add ground meat (break this up with a spoon when you add it in), tomatoes, chili beans, carrots, corn, red onion, chili seasoning, and garlic.
2. Cook for 4-6 hours on high in the slow cooker.
3. Stir well.
4. Serve with shredded cheese, sliced jalapeños, tortilla chips, sliced green onion, sliced jalapeños, and sour cream.

Autumn Sheet Pan

PREP TIME	COOK TIME	SERVINGS
15 mins	30 mins	8

INGREDIENTS

- 13 oz smoked turkey sausage
- 2 large sweet potatoes
- 8 oz brussels sprouts
- 1 red onion
- 2 tbsp garlic
- 2 apples

- Olive oil
- 2 tbsp dried thyme
- 2 tbsp dried sage
- 2 tbsp dried rosemary
- Fresh parsley

INSTRUCTIONS

1. Preheat oven to 400°F degrees. Spray a rimmed 18x13-inch baking sheet with non-stick cooking spray.
2. Add sliced sausage, diced sweet potatoes, brussel sprouts, diced apples, chopped onion and chopped garlic to sheet pan.
3. Drizzle everything with olive oil, sprinkle with thyme, sage and rosemary then season with salt and pepper to taste and toss to coat.
4. Roast in preheated oven 15 minutes then remove and toss.
5. Return to oven and continue to roast until veggies and apples are tender, about 15 minutes longer.
6. Sprinkle with parsley and serve warm.

White Chicken Chili

PREP TIME	COOK TIME	SERVINGS
15 mins	30 mins	8

INGREDIENTS

- 1 lb. ground chicken
- 1 package white chili seasoning
- 1 tablespoon chopped garlic
- ½ white onion, chopped
- 2 cans corn, drained

- 2 cans white chili beans, not drained
- 1 cup carrots, chopped
- Toppings: Sour cream, cilantro, tortilla chips, and shredded cheese if desired

INSTRUCTIONS

1. Add all ingredients besides toppings to the pressure cooker.
2. Cook on the Beans Chili setting.

3. Top with a sprinkle of shredded cheese, dollop of sour cream, sprinkle of cilantro if desired.
4. Serve with tortilla chips to dip. Enjoy!

Back-to-School Oatmeal Cups

PREP TIME	COOK TIME	SERVINGS
15 mins	25 mins	12

INGREDIENTS

- 2 large bananas, mashed
- 2 large eggs
- ¼ cup maple syrup
- 1 cup milk
- 1 tsp vanilla extract
- 2 cups rolled oats
- ½ cup flour
- 1 tsp baking powder
- 1 tsp ground cinnamon
- ¼ tsp salt

TOPPINGS
APPLE CINNAMON
- 3 tbsp finely diced apples
- Pinch of cinnamon

BLUEBERRY PUMPKIN
- 2 tbsp fresh blueberries
- 3 tbsp pumpkin puree

CHOCOLATE PUMPKIN BANANA
- 3 banana slices
- 3 tsp mini chocolate chips
- 3 tbsp pumpkin puree

INSTRUCTIONS

1. Preheat the oven to 350°F and generously spray muffin tin with non-stick cooking spray.
2. In a large bowl, mash banana. Add in eggs, maple syrup, milk and vanilla; mix to combine and set aside.
3. In another large bowl, mix together all of the dry ingredients.
4. Slowly add the wet ingredients to the dry ingredients. Mix until combined.
5. With a spoon, add batter to each muffin cup, filling each to close to the top. Add desired toppings to the top of each cup, pressing into the cup slightly to get some of the ingredients into the center of the muffins.
6. Bake for 20-23 minutes or until inserted toothpick comes out clean. Allow to cool before removing from muffin tin.

Chicken Quesadilla Soup

PREP TIME	COOK TIME	SERVINGS
10 mins	45 mins	8

INGREDIENTS

- 1 green bell pepper, diced
- ½ cup diced yellow onion
- 1 lb boneless skinless chicken breasts
- 1 can (10 oz) red enchilada sauce
- 1 can (10.5 oz) diced tomatoes with green chiles
- 2 cans (15 oz each) black beans, drained and rinsed
- 1 can (15 oz) southwestern corn (or regular sweet corn, or fire-roasted corn)
- 1 cup chicken stock or chicken broth

- 1 tbsp minced garlic
- 1 package (8 oz) full fat cream cheese, very softened
- ½ tsp ground cumin
- ¾ tsp paprika
- 1 tsp seasoned salt
- ¼ tsp pepper
- 1 ½ tbsp chili powder

INSTRUCTIONS

1. In pressure cooker, add in the diced green pepper, diced onion, uncooked chicken breasts, enchilada sauce, undrained tomatoes, drained and rinsed black beans, undrained corn, chicken stock or broth, minced garlic, and cream cheese.
2. Add in all of the seasonings: cumin, paprika, seasoned salt, pepper, and chilli powder. Stir well and cover.

3. Cook on high pressure cook setting.
4. Remove the chicken from Instant pot and shred using two forks.
5. Add the shredded chicken back into the Instant pot and stir.
6. Serve the soup bowls with sour cream, colby jack cheese, avocado, fresh lime, cilantro/green onions as desired.

Pumpkin Patch Brownies

PREP TIME	COOK TIME	SERVINGS
15 mins	35 mins	8

INGREDIENTS

BROWNIES
- 1 cup butter, melted and cooled
- 2 tbsp vegetable oil
- 1 ¼ cups white sugar
- 1 cup light brown sugar
- 4 eggs
- 1 tbsp pure vanilla extract
- ¾ tsp salt
- 1 cup flour
- 1 cup unsweetened cocoa powder

TOPPINGS
- 1 can of chocolate frosting
- Pumpkin candies

PUMPKIN SIGNS
- Popsicle sticks
- Glue
- Black marker

INSTRUCTIONS

1. Preheat oven to 350°F.
2. Lightly grease an 9x13-inch baking pan.
3. Combine melted butter, oil and sugars together in a medium-sized bowl. Whisk well.
4. Add the eggs and vanilla; beat another minute.
5. Sift in flour, cocoa powder and salt. Gently stir the dry ingredients into the wet ingredients until combined (do NOT over beat).
6. Pour batter into pan evenly. Bake for 30 minutes, until toothpick comes cleanly out of the center.
7. While brownies are baking, make pumpkin signs. Glue 4 popsicle sticks lengthwise to one popsicle stick. Once glue is dry, write "pumpkins 50¢" on signs with black magic marker.
8. Remove brownies from oven and let cool.
9. Cut off brownie crust, and cut brownies into squares. Top with chocolate frosting.
10. Crumble brownie crust and sprinkle on top to make "dirt".
11. Top each brownie with 2-3 candy pumpkins and a "pumpkin" sign.

Pumpkin Spice Lattes

PREP TIME	COOK TIME	SERVINGS
5 mins	5 mins	2

INGREDIENTS

- 2 cups of milk
- 3 tbsp of pure pumpkin puree
- 2-3 tbsp of sugar (depending on how sweet you want it)
- ½ tsp pumpkin pie spice blend, plus more for garnish

- 1 tbsp pure vanilla extract
- ½ cup of strong brewed coffee or hot espresso
- Sweetened whip cream
- Cinnamon sticks (for garnish)

INSTRUCTIONS

1. Combine the milk, pumpkin puree, sugar, pumpkin pie spice and vanilla extract in a saucepan.
2. Place over medium heat until hot, but don't boil.
3. Whisk milk mixture vigorously until it's foamy, about 30 seconds.

4. Pour coffee or espresso into 2 large mugs.
5. Divide the milk mixture and pour each half into the mugs.
6. Top with whipped cream. Add a sprinkle of pumpkin pie spice and cinnamon sticks for garnish.

I know everyone loves to get their PSLs from S-bucks, but I love the taste of this homemade one so much more! Happy pumpkin season!

Pumpkin Swirl Brownies

PREP TIME	COOK TIME	SERVINGS
20 mins	40 mins	8

INGREDIENTS

BROWNIE BATTER INGREDIENTS
- 1 box brownie mix
- 2 eggs
- ⅔ cup vegetable oil
- ¼ cup water

PUMPKIN SWIRL INGREDIENTS
- ½ cup pumpkin
- 3 tbsp sugar
- 1 egg
- 3 oz softened cream cheese
- 1 tsp ground cinnamon
- ¼ tsp nutmeg
- ¼ tsp pumpkin pie spice

INSTRUCTIONS

1. Preheat oven to 350°F.
2. Spray baking dish with cooking spray.
3. Mix brownie batter according to directions on box. In a separate bowl, mix the pumpkin swirl ingredients.
4. Pour half the brownie batter into baking dish.
5. Spoon pumpkin swirl over top of the brownie batter.
6. Add the remaining brownie batter.
7. With a knife, swirl the pumpkin and brownie batter by dragging knife top to bottom and left to right across the pan.
TIP: *The more swirls, the prettier it bakes!*
8. Bake 40 minutes, or until toothpick comes out clean.
9. Cool completely, cut, and serve. Enjoy!

Sparkling Cider

PREP TIME	COOK TIME	SERVINGS
15 mins	–	12

INGREDIENTS

- 2 apples, chopped with skins on
- ¼ tsp cinnamon
- ¼ tsp nutmeg
- 3 tbsp sugar
- 4 cups apple cider
- 1 cup sparkling white grape juice
- 2 cups sparkling cider
- 1 cup Sprite®
- 1 cup cranberries, for garnish
- 12 cinnamon sticks

INSTRUCTIONS

1. In a large pitcher mix fresh apple cider, Sprite®, sparkling cider, and sparkling white grape juice.
2. On a plate mix the sugar, cinnamon, and nutmeg.
3. Dip the rim of each glass in water (or in the sparkling cider) and then in the spiced sugar.
4. Add the diced apple pieces to the cups & pour your sparkling cider into each glass.
5. Garnish with a cinnamon stick and cranberries. Serve & enjoy.

Pumpkin Muffins

PREP TIME	COOK TIME	SERVINGS
15 mins	15 mins	12

INGREDIENTS

- 1 stick melted butter
- 1 cup milk
- 2 eggs
- ½ cup pumpkin
- 1 tsp vanilla
- ½ cup brown sugar
- 2 cups flour
- ½ cup oats
- 2 tsp baking soda

- 1 tsp pumpkin pie spice
- ½ cup white chocolate chips

TOPPING
- 4 tbsp melted butter
- 3 tbsp flour
- 2 tbsp brown sugar
- ½ tsp pumpkin pie spice

INSTRUCTIONS

1. Preheat oven to 400°F.
2. In large bowl, whisk together butter, milk, eggs, pumpkin, vanilla, and brown sugar.
3. Add in flour, oats, baking soda and pumpkin pie spice. Stir until combined.
4. Add in white chocolate chips. Stir until evenly mixed.
5. Scoop batter into muffin liners in muffin pans. Set aside.
6. In small bowl, mix the topping ingredients- melted butter, flour, brown sugar, and pumpkin pie spice.
7. Stir and sprinkle the top of each muffin with a little of the topping mixture.
8. Bake for 12 minutes. Let muffins cool
OPTIONAL: *Melt canned vanilla frosting in microwaveable bowl until liquified. With spoon, drizzle frosting over the top of muffins with a spoon.*

Autumn Potpourri

PREP TIME	COOK TIME	SERVINGS
10 mins	1 hour	-

INGREDIENTS

- 2 cups cranberries
- 1 sliced orange
- 1 sliced apple
- 2 cinnamon sticks
- 1 sprig of rosemary
- 5 cloves

- 5 anise stars
- 4 hazelnuts
- 2 drops bergamot oil
- 3 drops mandarin oil
- 4 - 6 cups of water

INSTRUCTIONS

1. Add all scented ingredients to a small cooking pot.
2. Cover with 4-6 cups of water, until ingredients are almost submerged.
3. Cook on medium heat until pot simmers. Reduce heat to low, and cook for one hour.

4. If you'd like to keep your potpourri on the stove for longer, add more water to keep ingredients almost submerged.

TIP: *If you'd like to use your potpouri over 2 days, turn off heat, and allow pot to cool completely. Add water to pot until ingredients are almost submerged. Refridgerate overnight, and reheat according to the day one instructions.*

Pumpkin Juice

PREP TIME	COOK TIME	SERVINGS
10 mins	10 mins	4 (8oz each)

INGREDIENTS

- 1 cup canned pumpkin
- 1 cup water
- ¼ cup sugar
- 1 cup sparkling cider or sparkling white wine
- 1 cup orange juice or apricot juice

RIM:
- 2 tbsp sugar
- 1 tbsp pumpkin spice
- Orange slice

INSTRUCTIONS

1. In a saucepan, mix pumpkin, water, and sugar until blended on low heat. Remove from heat and chill.
2. In a pitcher, mix pumpkin juice, sparkling cider/wine, and orange/apricot juice. Chill until serving time.

3. On a plate, mix 2 tbsp sugar and 1 tbsp pumpkin spice. Run an orange slice around the rim of your glass. Dip rim in the pumpkin spice mixture.
4. Pour pumpkin juice into 4 glasses and enjoy!

> Fun fact: my sister and I used to dress up as Hogwarts students for the HP movie premiers. The books and movies are my favorite– and it's so fun to make these drinks from the series. This one is in particular is SO refreshing! Cheers!

Butterbeer

PREP TIME
5 mins

COOK TIME
–

SERVINGS
1

INGREDIENTS

- 1 scoop vanilla ice cream
- 1 can cream soda OR bottle of butterscotch ale

- Whipped cream
- Butterscotch topping

INSTRUCTIONS

1. Add one scoop of vanilla ice cream to 16 oz. mason jar.
2. Pour cream soda or butterscotch ale over the ice cream.

3. Top with a dollop of whipped cream and drizzle with butterscotch topping.

THANKSGIVING

Thanksgiving was always my dad's favorite holiday, and it's become my favorite too.

There's something so magical about that official start of the Christmas season when you see Santa Claus waving at the end of the Thanksgiving Day Parade and enjoying a feast with your family. It was always our tradition to watch the parade together, and my dad would always take out the video camera to capture our faces when we saw Santa.

As a little girl, GG hosted our Thanksgiving dinners, and I loved helping her in the kitchen to put the finishing touches on the meal. No one can make mashed potatoes better than GG.

After we got married and moved to our current home, GG passed the torch and we host Thanksgiving dinner here. My mom taught me how to brine the turkey, which if you have not tried this, it always turns out amazing. I love turning on the parade in the morning while I'm prepping the food, and seeing the kids faces when they see characters they love float by. When they wave to Santa Claus with glee at the end of the parade, it feels just like when we were little.

THANKSGIVING

Thanksgiving Turkey Brine

PREP TIME	COOK TIME	SERVINGS
2 hours	24 hours	-

INGREDIENTS

- 3 cups apple cider
- 2 cups brown sugar
- 1 cup sea salt
- 3 tbsp multi-color peppercorns
- 5 whole bay leaves

- 2 heaping tbsp minced garlic
- 4 sprigs rosemary
- Rinds of three large oranges
- 1 turkey (this brine will work for any size turkey, but we host a lot of people, so I usually have a 20 lb turkey)
- 2 gallons of cold water

INSTRUCTIONS

1. Combine 2 gallons cold water with the apple cider, brown sugar, salt, peppercorns, bay leaves, garlic, rosemary and orange peels in a large pot.
2. Stir until the salt and sugar dissolve.
3. Bring to a boil, then turn off the heat and cover. Allow to cool completely-it usually takes about 1 to 1.5 hours to cool.
TIP: *I put mine outside, usually we have snow by then to chill.*

4. Put uncooked turkey in a large 5 gallon bucket. (I also use brine bucket liner for this.) Then pour the chilled brine solution over the turkey. Refrigerate for 16 to 24 hours.
TIP: *If you live in warmer weather, plan accordingly to fit the bucket in your fridge- it's big!*
5. When ready to roast the turkey, remove from the brine. Rinse turkey in cold water. Now you're ready for stuffing and baking the turkey!

Secret Family Stuffing

PREP TIME	COOK TIME	SERVINGS
90 mins	2-5 hours	24

INGREDIENTS

- 1 stick butter
- 5-6 celery stalks
- 1 yellow onion
- Turkey giblets
- 2 loaves stale wheat bread
- 2 eggs
- Salt + pepper

- 1 tbsp Old Bay seasoning
- 1 tbsp garlic powder

GRAVY
- ½ cup flour
- 1 tbsp cornstarch
- 2 cups turkey broth

INSTRUCTIONS

NOTE: *Break up your stuffing bread into one inch pieces and leave out overnight.*

1. Preheat oven to 350°F.
2. Chop onion and celery very finely.
3. Rinse your giblets and put in small pot with 2 cups water.
4. Bring to a boil and let it simmer for one hour.
5. After an hour, melt one stick of butter in large pan, add the celery and onion. Cook these until softened.
6. Add butter mixture to the bowl of bread, two eggs, salt and pepper, Old Bay seasoning, garlic powder and mix all together and slowly add in the water from the giblet pan (you might not use all of it- you just want your stuffing a little sticky).

7. Rinse the turkey, and set it breast up in the baking pan. Stuff the turkey with that stuffing! Any extra stuffing, put into a greased baking dish, refrigerate, and take out to bake for the last 30-45 minutes your turkey is in the oven.
8. Add giblets to the baking pan and ½ cup of water. Slice butter and add all over the top of the turkey.
9. Season with salt and pepper and cover with foil until last 30 minutes.
10. Bake at 350°F for 15 minutes per pound. Baste the turkey every 30 minutes. Temperature under thigh should be 185°F and stuffing and breast should be 165°F.
11. For your gravy, remove the giblets from the baking pan, whisk in turkey broth, corn starch, bring that to a simmer and keep warm until ready to serve!

Green Bean Casserole

PREP TIME
10 mins

COOK TIME
40 mins

SERVINGS
12

INGREDIENTS

- 1 (10 oz) can cream of mushroom soup
- ½ cup milk
- 1 cup shredded mozzarella cheese
- 1 tsp soy sauce
- 1 dash black pepper
- 2 cans (14.5 oz) French style green beans
- ⅔ cups French fried onion topping, keep rest of container for topping

INSTRUCTIONS

1. In a bowl, stir soup, milk, cheese, soy sauce, black pepper, beans and ⅔ cup onions together. Spread evenly in a 1 ½-quart casserole dish.
2. Bake at 350°F for 30 minutes or until the bean mixture is hot and bubbling.
3. Sprinkle with the remaining fried onions.
4. Bake for 10 minutes or until the onions are golden brown.

GG's Mashed Potatoes

PREP TIME	COOK TIME	SERVINGS
20 mins	20 mins	16

INGREDIENTS

- 8 restaurant potatoes
- 4-6 tbsp butter

- ⅓ cup milk (add more if you want creamier potatoes)
- Salt + pepper

INSTRUCTIONS

1. Wash and peel potatoes.
2. Cut into chunks and boil until tender.
3. Drain and mash potatoes.

4. Put in butter.
5. Add milk.
6. Add salt and pepper until you like the taste.
7. Mash until smooth.

No one can make mashed potatoes like GG can. This recipe is straight from her- and I have never tasted any better than hers!

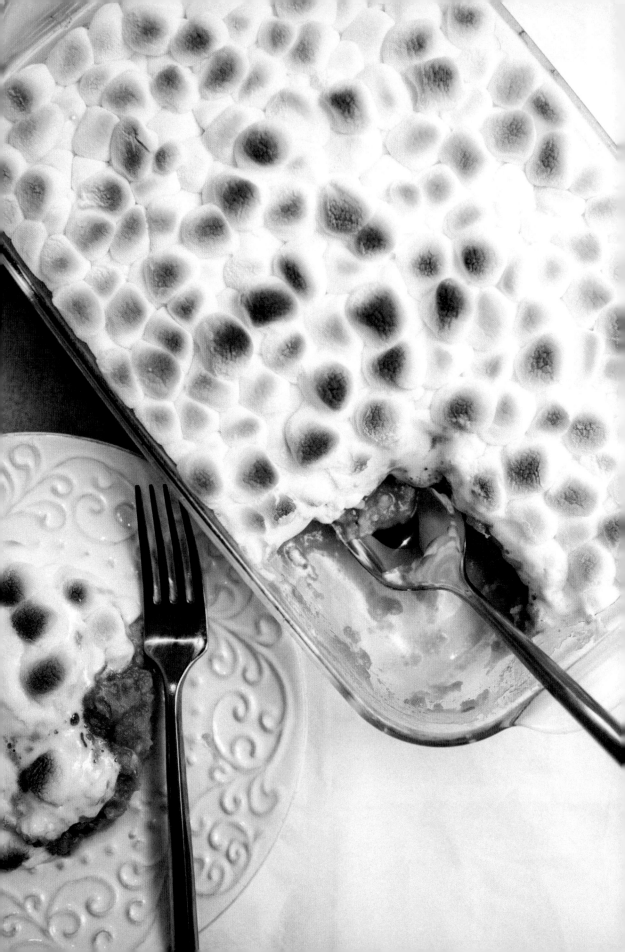

Sweet Potato Casserole

PREP TIME	COOK TIME	SERVINGS
10 mins	25 mins	12

INGREDIENTS

- 2 cans (29 oz) yams
- ¾ cup brown sugar
- ¼ cup butter, softened
- 1 ½ tsp salt
- ½ tsp vanilla extract
- ½ cup chopped pecans, optional
- Cooking spray
- 1 bag mini marshmallows

INSTRUCTIONS

1. While oven is preheating to 375°F, in a mixing bowl, mash the yams, sugar, butter, salt, vanilla, and pecans (optional).
2. Spray 13×9 baking dish with cooking spray and add in mashed mixture, spreading evenly in pan.
3. Bake for 15 minutes.
4. Remove pan from oven and top with a package of mini marshmallows.
5. Bake 10 minutes or until marshmallows are golden brown.

Cranberry Sauce

PREP TIME	**COOK TIME**	**SERVINGS**
5 mins	20 mins	12

INGREDIENTS

- 12 oz bag frozen cranberries
- 1 cup sugar
- ½ orange, juiced
- 1 tbsp lemon juice
- 2 tbsp water
- Salt + sugar to taste

INSTRUCTIONS

1. Reserve ½ cup frozen cranberries, and empty rest of the bag into a saucepan.
2. Add sugar, orange juice, lemon juice and water to the pan.
3. Cook over low heat for 10 minutes until the sugar dissolves and the cranberries are soft.
4. Increase the heat to medium and cook for 10 minutes, until the cranberries burst.
5. Reduce the heat to low and stir in the reserved cranberries.
6. Add sugar and salt to taste.
7. Cool to room temperature before serving.

Thanksgiving Sangria

PREP TIME	COOK TIME	SERVINGS
10 mins	–	8

INGREDIENTS

- 1 cup pomegranate juice
- 5 (3") cinnamon sticks
- 1 (750-ml) bottle red wine
- 1 (750-ml) bottle pear or apple sparkling cider
- 1 Bartlett pear, sliced thin
- ½ cup pomegranate seeds
- 1 orange, sliced
- Optional: Extra orange slices for garnish

INSTRUCTIONS

1. Fill pitcher with ice.
2. Pour sangria ingredients over ice.
3. Mix together.
4. Serve chilled with an orange garnish.

I made this sangria for our Friendsgiving, and everyone loved it! It went fast- and induced lots of laughter. It is the perfect sangria for any girls night or holiday gathering. Cheers!

Pumpkin Pie Cheesecake

PREP TIME	COOK TIME	SERVINGS
20 mins	40 mins	8

INGREDIENTS

PIE CRUST

- 1 ½ cups graham cracker crumbs
- ⅓ cup sugar
- 6 tbsp melted butter
- ½ tsp cinnamon

PIE FILLING

- 2 (8 oz) packages cream cheese
- ½ cup sugar
- 1 tsp vanilla extract
- 2 large eggs
- ½ cup pumpkin puree
- 2 tsp pumpkin spice
- Whipped cream

INSTRUCTIONS

1. Mix graham cracker crumbs, sugar, melted butter and cinnamon. Press mixture with your fingers into a pie plate (I use a 9-inch round).
2. Set cream cheese out to be at room temperature before blending.
3. Beat the cream cheese, sugar, vanilla, and eggs until smooth.
4. Add 1 ⅓ cups of the cheesecake batter to the pie crust.
5. Add pumpkin puree and pumpkin spice to the remaining cheesecake batter.
6. Blend until smooth.
7. Gently pour pumpkin batter on top of the plain cheesecake layer - do not mix.
8. Bake at 325°F for 35 to 40 minutes.
9. Let cool for one hour and refrigerate overnight.
10. Top with whipped cream right before serving.

Green Bean Casserole Queso

PREP TIME	COOK TIME	SERVINGS
10 mins	20 mins	12

INGREDIENTS

- 1 (15 oz) jar of queso
- 1 cup of shredded pepper jack or taco cheese
- Leftover green bean casserole (see recipe on pg. 103)
- ½ cup French fried onions topping

INSTRUCTIONS

1. Spread half the jar of queso in a 9x9 baking dish.
2. Scoop on the green bean casserole.
3. Pour other half of queso on top of casserole.
4. Sprinkle cheese and onions on top of the queso.
5. Pop it in the oven at 350°F for 15 minutes.
6. Broil 3 minutes, until top is brown and bubbly.
7. Serve warm with tortilla chips to dip.

> On Black Friday, we don't go shopping. Instead, we always get a live Christmas tree and decorate it, while enjoying Thanksgiving leftovers. This has been a family tradition since I was little. And I love making this queso with leftover green bean casserole! Warning: it is addicting!

CHRISTMAS BRUNCH

Every Christmas morning as a child, when we were finished opening our presents, we would sit down for this meal with my grandparents and great aunt and uncle, usually still in our Christmas pajamas.

The house would be filled with the smell of freshly baked cinnamon rolls, orange juice, bacon, and breakfast sausage. I remember hearing my mom and gramma in the kitchen chatting while they put the finishing touches on brunch. My poppy leading us in prayer before we'd eat. My Uncle Jim taking extra helpings of the raspberries for the Lemon Bavarian Ice.

My mom always told me she got these recipes from my lovely Aunt Charlene, my dad's older sister.

When I remake this brunch for my family on Christmas Day, it takes me back to childhood Christmases, full of love and laughter. Now I love thinking about the Christmas mornings when Landon and Presley's cheeks were all sticky from the cinnamon rolls, and I cannot wait to keep making this meal for years to come as our family grows. I hope you feel all the Christmas joy through these special recipes. Merry Christmas!

CHRISTMAS BRUNCH

Lemon Bavarian Ice

PREP TIME	COOK TIME	SERVINGS
20 mins	overnight	12

INGREDIENTS

- 1 (6 oz) package of lemon gelatin
- 2 cups boiling water
- 4 cups ice cubes

- 1 (10 oz). container of whipped topping
- 1 (12 oz) package of frozen raspberries

INSTRUCTIONS

1. In a large bowl, dissolve gelatin into boiling water.
2. Add ice cubes and stir until thickened to consistency of egg whites. Discard any remaining ice.
3. Put Cool Whip® into large mixing bowl. Gently fold gelatin into whipped topping, using a large whisk.
4. Pour into a generous 2 quart mold (ours growing up was wreath shaped), and chill overnight.
5. Unmold, slice, and serve with raspberries on top.
TIP: *If you don't have a mold, you could pour the gelatin into wine glasses or mason jars to make individual sized servings!*

Sausage Breakfast Casserole

PREP TIME	COOK TIME	SERVINGS
30 mins	1 hour 15 mins	12

INGREDIENTS

- 2.5 lbs mild Italian sausage
- 15 slices wheat bread
- 2 cups shredded colby jack or cheddar cheese
- 4 eggs
- 2 ¼ cups milk
- Salt + pepper
- 1 (10 oz) can cream of mushroom soup

INSTRUCTIONS

1. Tear up bread into 1 inch pieces and spread into 13×9 baking dish.
2. Brown and cook the sausage on medium heat until browned. Drain, and let cool. Slice the sausage into bite size pieces. Sprinkle evenly over the bread.
3. Sprinkle the cheese evenly over the sausage and bread.
4. Spread can of mushroom soup over the top.
5. Beat 4 eggs and milk with a whisk, add salt and pepper, and pour evenly over casserole.
6. Cover with tin foil, and refrigerate overnight.
7. Bake in the morning, leaving tin foil covering on, at 375°F for 1 hour. Take foil off, and bake for 15 more minutes at 350°F until top is golden brown.
8. Take out of oven, and let cool for 30 minutes before serving.

Cinnamon Rolls

PREP TIME	COOK TIME	SERVINGS
2 hours 20 mins	20 mins	12

INGREDIENTS

CINNAMON ROLL DOUGH

- 1 cup milk
- 1 tbsp sugar
- 1 tbsp active dry yeast
- 2 large eggs
- ½ cup sugar
- 6 tbsp butter, melted
- 1 tsp pure vanilla extract
- 4 cups all-purpose flour
- 1 tsp salt
- 1 tsp ground cinnamon

CINNAMON SUGAR FILLING

- 1 cup brown sugar
- 3 tbsp cinnamon
- 8 tbsp butter, softened

CREAM CHEESE FROSTING

- 1 (8 oz) package cream cheese, softened
- ¼ cup butter, softened
- 2 cups powdered sugar
- 1 tsp pure vanilla extract
- ¼ tsp salt

INSTRUCTIONS

DOUGH

1. Warm milk in the microwave for 45 seconds.
2. In mixer, add milk, then add 1 tbsp sugar and yeast to the warm milk. Stir and let it sit for five minutes or until it becomes foamy.
3. Add ½ cup sugar, butter, eggs, and vanilla to the mixture in the bowl.
4. Add 4 cups flour, salt and cinnamon, slowly increasing speed to high.
5. Knead dough until a large ball is formed. The dough should be smooth. If the dough seems sticky, add more flour 1 tbsp at a time until smooth.
6. Transfer dough to a floured surface and knead with your hands for 3-5 minutes until smooth. Form into a ball. Place dough inside a large greased bowl. Cover the bowl with a warm, damp towel. Put the bowl in a warm place to rise for about 1 hour. While the dough is rising, make the filling.

FILLING

7. In a small bowl, combine butter, brown sugar and cinnamon until mixture is smooth. Set aside.

8. When dough has risen, sprinkle a large work surface with flour. Gently press the bubbles out of the dough and form it into a rectangle. Roll the dough into a 24 inch x 12 inch rectangle, about ¼ inch thick.
9. Spread the filling all over the dough. Roll up dough. Cut into 12 equal sized rolls - each roll ~2 inches long.
10. Line a 9x13 glass baking dish with parchment paper and lightly grease. Then place rolls in 4 rows of three, evenly spaced. Cover and let rise for ~30 minutes. Cinnamon rolls should double in size.
11. Preheat the oven to 350°F. Bake cinnamon rolls for 18-20 minutes.

FROSTING

12. Beat together cream cheese, butter, powdered sugar, vanilla extract and salt. Keep frosting at room temperature until the cinnamon rolls are baked.
13. Once the cinnamon rolls are removed from the oven, spread the cream cheese frosting on them while they are still warm, or pop frosting in microwave for 30-45 seconds to melt slightly, and use a spoon to drizzle over the top of the cinnamon rolls.

Kiwi Tree

PREP TIME	COOK TIME	SERVINGS
15 mins	-	12

INGREDIENTS

- 5 kiwis
- ½ pint raspberries

- 1 starfruit

INSTRUCTIONS

1. Remove skin of kiwis and slice thinly.
2. Reserve skin in rectangle shape for tree trunk.
3. Put sliced kiwi in shape of tree on clear or white platter.

4. Decorate the trees with raspberries.
5. Place a slice of starfruit on top of tree.

> I first hosted Christmas brunch the year we moved into our home. My mom brought this over– it was not part of our brunch growing up, but the kids and I absolutely loved it! It's been a nice new addition to brunch ever since!

Christmas Mimosas

PREP TIME	COOK TIME	SERVINGS
10 mins	–	8

INGREDIENTS

- 1 lime, sliced
- 2 tbsp gold or red color sugar crystals
- 1 (52 oz) bottle orange juice
- 1 (750 ml) bottle of Champagne
- Fruit for garnish- oranges, frozen cranberries, pomegranate, or raspberries

INSTRUCTIONS

1. Place sugar crystals on a small plate. Rim champagne glass in lime juice then immediately dip in sugar crystals.
2. Fill glass with half juice and half champagne.

3. Garnish with fruit. I like adding a wedge of orange, or dropping frozen cranberries, pomegranate, or raspberries into the mimosa for some extra color!

Cranberry Cosmo

PREP TIME	COOK TIME	SERVINGS
10 mins	–	2

INGREDIENTS

- 2 shots (3 oz) raspberry vodka
- 2 shots (3 oz) of triple sec
- 4 oz. cranberry juice
- Ice
- Juice squeezed from ½ a lime
- 1 sprig of rosemary
- Frozen cranberries
- 2 tbsp red sugar crystals

INSTRUCTIONS

1. Pour vodka, triple sec, cranberry juice, and lime juice in shaker with ice.
2. Shake well.
3. Pour sugar crystals on a plate. With a lime wedge, rim 2 martini glasses with lime, and dip into sugar crystals immediately.
4. Pour cocktail into sugared glasses.
5. Garnish with ½ a sprig of rosemary and frozen cranberries.

Peppermint Pie

PREP TIME	REFRIGERATION TIME	SERVINGS
50 mins	overnight	8

INGREDIENTS

- 1 (6 oz) oreo pie crust
- 1 (10 oz) bag marshmallows
- ½ cup milk
- 1 (11 oz) bag white chocolate chips
- 1 tsp vanilla
- 3 drops peppermint extract
- 6 drops red dye
- 4 tbsp crushed peppermint candy
- 1 ½ cups whipped cream

INSTRUCTIONS

1. In a saucepan, combine marshmallows, white chocolate chips, and milk over low heat. Cook and stir until marshmallows are melted and mixture is smooth. Remove from heat.

2. Stir in vanilla, peppermint extract and food coloring. Cool 30 minutes, stirring every 10 minutes. Stir in 2 tablespoons crushed candies. Fold in 1 cup whipped cream (keep extra for topping).

3. Pour into oreo pie crust.

4. Refrigerate overnight.

5. Top with whipped cream and crushed peppermint candy before serving.

Christmas Tree Cake

PREP TIME	COOK TIME	SERVINGS
20 mins	30 mins	8

INGREDIENTS

- 2 ¼ cups flour
- 1 tsp baking powder
- 1 tsp baking soda
- ½ tsp salt
- 2 ½ tsp ground cinnamon
- 1 tsp nutmeg
- 1 tsp ground ginger
- ½ tsp allspice
- ¾ cups light-brown sugar
- ¾ cup vegetable oil

- ¾ cup applesauce
- 4 large eggs
- 2 tsp vanilla extract
- 1 cup milk

DECORATIONS
- 1 can cream cheese frosting
- 10 sprigs of rosemary
- 6-10 cranberries
- 1 tbsp pomegranate seeds

INSTRUCTIONS

1. Preheat oven to 350°F. Grease two 9-inch round baking pans.

2. In a mixing bowl, whisk together flour, baking powder, baking soda, salt, cinnamon, nutmeg, ginger, allspice, and set aside.

3. Pour brown sugar into the bowl of an electric mixer. Break up brown sugar with fingertips until no clumps remain. Pour in vegetable oil and applesauce, and blend until well combined.

4. Mix in eggs and vanilla. Add in ½ of the flour mixture and mix on low speed until combined, then blend in milk, and add remaining flour mixture. Mix until well combined.

5. Divide batter evenly among two baking pans. Bake for 30 minutes.

6. Cool completely. Level tops of cakes as needed. Frost with cream cheese frosting

7. Layer rosemary sprigs in shape of a Christmas tree.

8. Decorate tree with cranberries and pomegranate seed "ornaments."

Christmas Potpourri

PREP TIME	COOK TIME	SERVINGS
10 mins	60 mins	-

INGREDIENTS

- 2 cups cranberries
- 1 orange, sliced
- 2 cinnamon sticks
- 1-3 sprigs of rosemary

- 4-6 cups water (fill to just above where the ingredients lay in the pot)
- 3 drops bergamot oil
- 3 drops mandarin oil

INSTRUCTIONS

1. In a small cooking pot, add cranberries, sliced orange, cinnamon sticks, and rosemary.
2. Fill pot with water until just about where the ingredients lay in the pot.

3. Add in drops of essential oils.
4. Heat on medium, until bubbling. Reduce heat to low and simmer for 1 hour.

CHRISTMAS COOKIES

During the most magical time of the year, nothing tastes more like Christmas or smells better to me than homemade Christmas cookies.

Every year as a little girl, we'd have cookie baking days, where we'd make batch after batch of the recipes in this section to pass out to neighbors, family, and friends. My mom has a wonderful voice, so we'd always play the Time Life Treasury of Christmas album, and sing along during our cookie baking marathon.

I remember my mom would buy those huge plastic storage bins that were long - the kind that could slide under your bed - to store all the cookies we would bake.

After one of our baking days, we left the house to do some Christmas shopping. While we were gone, our dog, a fluffy white Bichon named Bianca, broke out of the gates to keep her in the kitchen, climbed up on the dining room table, and got into one of the plastic storage bins of cookies. She ate the ENTIRE container! Luckily, she survived (she actually lived to be 18), but it goes to show these cookies are irresistible to anyone or anything who smells them! So I hope you enjoy every single one of these recipes, from our family to yours!

CHRISTMAS COOKIES

Butter Cookies

PREP TIME	COOK TIME	SERVINGS
45 mins	10 mins	2 dozen

INGREDIENTS

- ½ lb (2 sticks) margarine
- 1 cup powdered sugar
- 1 egg
- 1 ½ tsp real almond extract
- 1 tsp vanilla extract
- 2 ½ cups flour
- 1 (16 oz) can vanilla or cream cheese frosting
- Assorted sprinkles

INSTRUCTIONS

1. Cream margarine, powdered sugar, egg, almond, and vanilla together. Then mix in flour.
2. Push dough into a smooth ball in mixing bowl. Cover in plastic wrap, and chill dough for 30 minutes
3. Roll out dough on lightly floured surface.
Tip from my mom: Roll dough to medium thickness (about ¼ inch) so they are chewy- too thin they will break easily.
4. Dip your cookie cutters in flour before cutting the dough. Put cut cookies on non-greased baking pan.
5. Bake at 350°F for 8-10 minutes. Let cool.
6. Frost with vanilla or cream cheese frosting and sprinkles of your choice. I love letting the kids do this part.

Mulac Kolachies

PREP TIME	COOK TIME	SERVINGS
45 mins	10 mins	2 dozen

INGREDIENTS

- 3 egg yolks
- ½ pint sour cream
- ½ lb (2 sticks) margarine
- 3 cups flour
- 1 tsp baking powder
- Pinch of salt
- 1 tsp vanilla
- Fruit filling, fruit preserves, or pie filling (we always used cherry, apricot, raspberry, nut, prune, and poppyseed)

INSTRUCTIONS

1. Blend flour, butter, baking powder, and salt.
2. Mix yolks with sour cream and add to flour mixture.
3. Add vanilla.
4. Roll semi-thin (⅛ inch thick) and cut into squares (these puff up, so you don't want them too thick).
5. Fold all corners to meet in the center. Brush the tops with egg whites.
6. Bake on ungreased cookie sheet at 350°F for 10 minutes until brown.
7. After they've cooled, sprinkle with powdered sugar.
8. Store in airtight container.

Maple Thumbprints

PREP TIME	COOK TIME	SERVINGS
25 mins	10 mins	2 dozen

INGREDIENTS

- ⅔ cup maple syrup
- 1 stick margarine, softened
- 3 oz cream cheese, softened
- 1 egg
- 2 cups flour
- 1 ⅓ cups chopped walnuts (optional)

- 1 tsp baking powder
- 1 tsp baking soda
- ¼ tsp salt
- Fruit filling, fruit preserves, or pie filling (we like cherry, apricot, and raspberry)

INSTRUCTIONS

1. Beat margarine, cream cheese, and egg until smooth.
2. Add in syrup and blend until smooth.
3. Add dry ingredients, and mix well.
4. Chill dough for 10 minutes.
5. Remove from refrigerator and roll into 1 inch balls. Place on ungreased cookie sheet.
6. Press center with thumb or knuckle. Fill with thumbprint with fruit filling.
7. Bake 10 minutes at 350°F until edges are golden brown.
8. Cool completely.
9. Sprinkle with powdered sugar.
10. Store in airtight container.

TIP FROM MY MOM: Double this recipe, as it makes about 2 dozen cookies and they go fast!

I love all our Christmas cookies, but these have grown to be my very favorite! Especially with raspberry filling!

Italian White Cookies

PREP TIME	COOK TIME	SERVINGS
30 mins	10 mins	4 dozen

INGREDIENTS

- 8 cups flour
- 8 tsp baking powder
- 2 cups sugar
- 1 lb (4 sticks) margarine
- 6 eggs
- ½ pt sour cream
- 1 ½ tsp vanilla

ICING
- 1 cup powdered sugar
- ⅓ cup milk
- Rainbow or Christmas colored nonpareils sprinkles

INSTRUCTIONS

1. In large bowl, mix flour, baking powder, sugar, margarine and put aside.
2. In a separate bowl, beat eggs until fluffy. Add sour cream and vanilla.
3. Make a well in flour mix and pour liquid in. Mix in well.
4. Knead until dough becomes smooth.
5. Break off little pieces at a time, and roll into shapes of S, 1, or 8.
7. Put cookies on ungreased cookie sheet.
8. Bake at 350°F for 8-10 minutes. Let cool.
9. Mix together powdered sugar and milk. Frost with a brush. Make sure you add your sprinkles before the icing dries.

Peanut Butter Cookies

PREP TIME
15 mins

COOK TIME
15 mins

SERVINGS
2 dozen

INGREDIENTS

- ½ lb (2 sticks) margarine softened
- ½ cup peanut butter
- 1 egg
- 2 tbsp milk
- 1 tsp vanilla
- ½ cup sugar

- ½ cup brown sugar
- 1 ¾ cup flour
- 1 tsp baking soda
- ½ tsp salt
- 1 package chocolate kisses

INSTRUCTIONS

1. Sift flour, baking soda and salt together. Set aside.
2. In a separate bowl, cream butter and peanut butter. Add egg, milk, vanilla, sugar, and brown sugar. Cream well.
3. Blend in dry ingredients gradually.

4. Shape into 1 inch balls and roll in sugar.
TIP: You can use colored sugar crystals to be festive!
5. Bake at 350°F on ungreased cookie sheet for 8 minutes.
6. Remove cookies from oven, and place an unwrapped chocolate kiss in center.
7. Bake for 5 more minutes.

Snowballs

PREP TIME	COOK TIME	SERVINGS
45 mins	15 mins	2 dozen

INGREDIENTS

- 1 cup butter
- ½ cup powdered sugar
- 1 tsp vanilla

- 2 ¼ cup flour
- ¼ tsp salt
- ¾ cup chopped walnut

INSTRUCTIONS

1. Cream together butter, sugar, vanilla, and salt.
2. Gradually add flour in. Lastly, stir in the nuts and mix well.
3. Chill dough for 30 minutes.
4. Remove dough from refrigerator and scoop dough out with a 1 tablespoon measure. Roll in balls.

5. Bake at 350°F for 10-12 minutes on an ungreased cookie sheet.
6. Remove from oven. While still warm, roll in powdered sugar.
7. Store in airtight container.

DESSERTS + DRINKS

Let's end on a sweet note, with some of our favorite desserts and drinks.

Landon and Presley both love desserts, but Presley has got the biggest sweet tooth. Many of these recipes I make and think of her - because she will always ask to help me to make cookies or dump cake. She just loves helping me no matter what I'm cooking, but especially if I'm baking, she always asks to join.

Most of the time, some ingredients get spilled out on the counter, so I've gotten good at eye-balling to make sure these recipes turn out- but I wouldn't trade the messes for anything. Getting to bake with my babies brings me so much joy, and ultimately was one of the reasons I had to write this cookbook.

When I think of all the memories I made with my family growing up over the meals in this book, and how special it was for my mom to pass along the recipes and all her tips and tricks, I want to do the same for my kids so that one day they can pass along these recipes too.

It means the world to share this cookbook with you.

DESSERTS + DRINKS

Apple Berry Crumble

PREP TIME	COOK TIME	SERVINGS
15 mins	40 mins	8

INGREDIENTS

- ¾ cup flour
- ½ cup oats
- ½ cup sugar
- Pinch of salt
- 1 cup butter - 3/4 cup melted, 1/4 cup sliced

- 5 apples (any kind will do!)
- 2 cups mixed berries (fresh or frozen)
- 2 tbsp lemon juice
- 2 tbsp brown sugar

INSTRUCTIONS

1. Preheat the oven to 350°F.
2. Core and dice the apples (I keep the skins on).
3. Add to greased 13x9 baking dish.
4. Add berries on the top of the apples in baking dish.
5. Sprinkle with the brown sugar and drizzle with the lemon juice.

6. In a separate large bowl, mix flour, sugar, oats and salt and mix to combine. Add butter, and mix with hands to form a crumbly mixture.
7. Cover the fruit with the crumble. Top with slices of the 1/4 cup of butter.
8. Bake for 40 minutes, until the top is golden and fruit is bubbling.
9. Serve warm with whipped cream or ice cream. Refrigerate leftovers or if not serving immediately.

> *I love making this recipe after going apple picking in the fall! You can use any kind of apples– and it always tastes amazing when they're fresh picked!*

Frog's Eye Salad

COOK TIME	REFRIGERATION TIME	SERVINGS
40 mins	overnight, +2 hours	20

INGREDIENTS

- 1 cup sugar
- 1 tbsp flour
- 2 ½ tsp salt
- 1 ¾ cup pineapple juice
- 2 eggs (beaten)
- 1 tbsp lemon juice
- 3 qts water
- 1 tbsp cooking oil

- 1 (16 oz) package acini de pepe
- 3 (11 oz) cans mandarin oranges (drained)
- 2 (20 oz) cans pineapple tidbits (drained)
- 1 (20 oz) can crushed pineapple (drained)
- 1 (9 oz) carton whipped topping
- 1 cup mini marshmallows (optional)
- 1 cup coconut (opitonal)

INSTRUCTIONS

1. Combine sugar, flour and ½ tsp salt in a sauce pan.
2. Gradually stir in pineapple juice and eggs.
3. Cook over moderate heat, stirring until thickened.
4. Add lemon juice, cool mixture to room temperature.
5. In a separate large pot, bring water, remaining 2 tsp salt and oil to a boil.
6. Add acini de pepe. Cook uncovered at a rolling boil until done.
7. Drain and rinse with water, cool to room temp.
8. Combine egg mixture and acini de pepe.
9. Refrigerate overnight in airtight container.
10. The next day, add oranges, pineapple, marshmallows and whipped topping.
11. Mix lightly but thoroughly.
12. Refrigerate at least 2 hours.
13. May be refreigerated for as long as one week.

Weirdest name for a really yummy dessert! The acini de pepe noodles give this salad its name, but it is one my sister and cousins always beg GG to make. It is delicious!

Dump Cake

PREP TIME	**COOK TIME**	**SERVINGS**
5 mins	40 mins	12

INGREDIENTS

- 1 (20 oz) can of crushed pineapple
- 1 (20 ox) can of cherry pie filling

- 1 stick of butter
- 1 box of yellow cake mix

INSTRUCTIONS

1. Spray 13x9 baking dish with cooking spray.
2. Dump in crushed pineapple and spread evenly.
3. Pour in cherry filling and spread evenly.
4. Sprinkle the cake mix over the filling.

5. Place slices of butter all over the cake.
6. Bake at 350°F for 40 minutes, until light golden brown.
7. Can be served warm a la mode with ice cream, or served when cooled. Refrigerate leftovers.

Apple Pie Cups

PREP TIME	COOK TIME	SERVINGS
10 mins	20 mins	8

INGREDIENTS

- Cooking spray
- 1 ⅓ cups apple pie filling
- 1 can cinnamon rolls with buttercream icing
- Ground cinnamon

INSTRUCTIONS

1. Heat oven to 375°F. Spray 8 regular-size muffin cups with cooking spray.
2. Separate dough into 8 rolls. Press each piece into and up sides of muffin cup into a cup form.
3. Chop up the apples in the pie filling. Spoon 2 generous tablespoons of filling into each dough-lined cup.
4. Bake for 14 to 18 minutes or until golden brown; cool in pan 5 minutes.
5. Transfer icing to small microwavable bowl.
6. Microwave uncovered until thin enough to drizzle (about 10 seconds).
7. Place rolls on serving plate; drizzle icing over rolls with a spoon.
8. Serve warm.
9. Sprinkle cinnamon on the pie cups for extra flavor.

Bunny Dirt Cake

PREP TIME	**COOK TIME**	**SERVINGS**
30 mins	35 mins	12

INGREDIENTS

- 1 box of chocolate cake mix
- 3 eggs
- 1 cup water
- ½ cup vegetable oil
- 1 (10 oz) bag white chocolate melting wafers
- Orange food coloring
- 9-12 large strawberries
- 1 (16 oz) can chocolate frosting
- 1 (17 oz) box chocolate cream cookies

INSTRUCTIONS

1. Rinse strawberries and dry well. Set aside so they become room temperature.
2. Mix chocolate cake according to directions on the box. Bake in a 13×9 baking dish according to package instructions.
3. Melt white chocolate wafers in a glass bowl over a pot of boiling water, stirring every 30-60 seconds
4. Once melted, add orange food coloring and mix until color is evenly dispersed.
5. Coat strawberries with orange chocolate up until the green crown, giving the appearance of a carrot. Cool on wax paper on a plate.
TIP: *You can sprinkle with orange sugar too*
6. Frost cake with chocolate frosting
7. Crush up the container of chocolate cookies
8. Sprinkle crushed cookies on top of frosting
9. Top with chocolate covered strawberry "carrots"
10. Cut into squares and serve. Refrigerate if not serving immediately.

Easter Peep Cookies

PREP TIME	COOK TIME	SERVINGS
1 hour	10 mins	24

INGREDIENTS

Cookies
- 2 ½ cups flour
- 1 cup powdered sugar
- 1 ½ tsp real almond extract
- 1 tsp real vanilla extract
- 2 sticks margarine
- 1 egg

Icing
- ½ cup powdered sugar, sifted
- ⅛ tsp real almond extract
- 1-2 tsp milk or water
- ½ tsp powdered food coloring OR 5-10 drops liquid food coloring (we use yellow, pink, and purple)

INSTRUCTIONS

COOKIES
1. Cream everything together but the flour. Mix in flour last.
2. Refrigerate dough for 30 minutes to 1 hour.
3. Roll out on lightly floured surface. TIP: Roll to medium thickness (about ¼ inch- if they are too thin they break easily).
4. Dip your bunny cookie cutter in flour before cutting the dough.
5. Bake at 350°F for 8-10 minutes. Let cool completely.
6. Frost with sugar cookie icing.

ICING
1. Sift powdered sugar. Then add wet ingredients right before you are about to ice cookies when they are completely cooled.
2. Whisk together.
3. Use brushes to paint on icing.
4. Immediately add sugar crystal sprinkles.
OPTIONAL: Add 3 dots of chocolate icing for the eyes and noses of the bunnies.

Strawberry Pretzel Salad

PREP TIME	REFRIGERATION TIME	SERVINGS
1 hour	overnight	12

INGREDIENTS

- 2 cups crushed pretzels
- ¾ cup butter, melted
- 3 tbsp sugar
- 1 (8 oz) package cream cheese, softened
- 1 cup white sugar

- 1 (8 oz) container frozen whipped topping, thawed
- 2 (3 oz) packages of strawberry flavored gelatin
- 2 cups boiling water
- 2 (10 oz) packages frozen strawberries

INSTRUCTIONS

1. Preheat oven to 400°F.
2. Stir together crushed pretzels, melted butter and 3 tbsp sugar.
3. Mix well and press mixture into bottom of a greased 9x13 baking dish.
4. Bake 8 to 10 minutes, until set. Set aside to cool.
5. In a large bowl, cream together cream cheese and 1 cup sugar.
6. Fold in whipped topping. Spread mixture onto cooled crust.
7. Dissolve gelatin in boiling water. Stir in frozen strawberries and allow to set briefly.
8. When about the consistency of egg whites, pour and spread over cream cheese layer.
9. Refrigerate overnight.
10. Remove from refrigerator. Cut into squares and serve cool.

> This is another dessert from GG. Every year at her church, there was a women's salad luncheon, where everyone would bring in a salad and exchange recipes. This Strawberry Pretzel "Salad" was always a hit!

S'mores Lasagna

PREP TIME	**REFRIGERATION TIME**	**SERVINGS**
30 mins	2 hours	12

INGREDIENTS

- ¼ cup cocoa powder
- 2 (4 oz) packages of chocolate pudding
- 3 ½ cups milk
- 2 (8 oz) blocks of cream cheese
- 1 (7 oz) jar marshmallow creme
- 2 sleeves of graham crackers

- 2 cups chocolate chips
- 1 (16 oz) container of whipped topping
- 4 cups mini marshmallows
- 8-10 miniature chocolate bars
- Hot fudge
- ½ cup crushed graham crackers

INSTRUCTIONS

1. In a large bowl, combine chocolate pudding, cocoa, and milk. Mix together until blended into pudding texture. Put in fridge until ready to make lasagna layers.
2. In another bowl, beat marshmallow crème with cream cheese until smooth.
3. Spray 13x9 pan with cooking spray. Layer graham crackers, then marshmallow cream cheese mixture. Top with 1 cup mini marshmallows, then cover with chocolate pudding and a third of the chocolate chips. Repeat 2 times.
4. Cover and refrigerate for 2 hours.
5. Remove lasagna from refrigerator. Top with whipped topping.
6. Sprinkle with crushed graham crackers, 1 cup mini marshmallows, and miniature chocolate bars.
7. Heat hot fudge sauce in the microwave so it is just pourable but not too hot (about 30 seconds). Drizzle hot fudge all over lasagna with a spoon.
8. Cut in squares and serve immediately.

Ombre Heart Cookies

INGREDIENTS

COOKIES

- 2 ½ cups flour
- 1 cup powdered sugar
- 1 ½ tsp real almond extract
- 1 tsp real vanilla extract
- 2 sticks margarine
- 1 egg

LEMON RASPBERRY OMBRÉ FROSTING:

- 4 oz cream cheese, softened
- 12 tbsp of butter, softened
- 3 cups powdered sugar
- 3 tbsp freeze dried raspberry powder (buy freeze dried raspberries and crush into a powder)
- 1 tbsp lemon juice

INSTRUCTIONS

COOKIES

1. Cream everything together but the flour. Mix in flour last.
2. Refrigerate dough for 30 minutes to 1 hour.
3. Roll out on lightly floured surface. TIP: Roll to medium thickness (about 1/4 inch- if they are too thin they break easily)
4. Dip your heart cookie cutter in flour before cutting the dough.
5. Bake at 350°F for 8-10 minutes. Let cool completely.
6. Frost with lemon raspberry ombre frosting.

FROSTING

1. Cream together the cream cheese and butter with an electric mixer until smooth.
2. Add lemon juice and the powdered sugar, one cup at a time until fluffy and creamy.
3. Add a sprinkle of the raspberry powder and decorate the first few cookies.
4. Add a little more raspberry powder and decorate a few more, gradually adding more powder to each batch, creating a gradual darker pink.

Vanilla Bean Lemonade

PREP TIME	REFRIGERATION TIME	SERVINGS
20 mins	1 hour	4

INGREDIENTS

- ½ cup granulated sugar
- 1 cup + 3 cups water (divided)
- 1 vanilla bean (sliced open and seeds scraped)

- ½ cup fresh-squeezed lemon juice
- Ice for serving

INSTRUCTIONS

1. Add the sugar and 1 cup water to a medium saucepan over medium heat.
2. Slice the vanilla bean open with a paring knife and scrape the seeds from the bean and add to the saucepan along with the remaining whole bean.
3. Heat, stirring occasionally, until the mixture begins to steam and the sugar has dissolved, about 3-4 minutes.
4. Remove from heat and set aside for 15 minutes.

5. Meanwhile, add remaining 3 cups water and lemon juice to a pitcher. Pour through a sieve into the pitcher the vanilla/sugar mixture. Discard solids.
6. Stir well and chill for 1 hour.
7. Fill individual glasses with ice and pour lemonade over the ice.

Summer Sangria

PREP TIME
10 mins

REFRIGERATION TIME
2 hours

SERVINGS
8

INGREDIENTS

- 1 bottle sweet white wine (750 ml)
- 1 cup watermelon vodka
- 1 lime, thinly sliced

- 2 cups watermelon, cubed and cold
- 2 cups cold lemon lime soda
- Ice cubes

INSTRUCTIONS

1. Pour the wine, vodka, and soda into a pitcher and stir to combine. Add the sliced lime and watermelon.
2. To serve, place a few sliced limes and water melon cubes into a glass with ice. Pour the sangria over the ice.

TIP: *The sangria can be made up to 2 hours before serving but can be served immediately.*

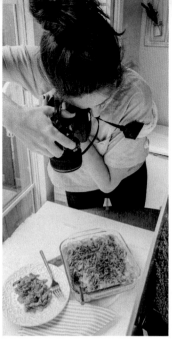

ACKNOWLEDGEMENTS

I feel incredibly blessed that God gave me the motivation and the team needed to make publishing this cookbook possible. Thank you Jesus!

On a team call in August, we decided to make my cookbook dream a reality. This would not have been possible without Molly Watson, Morgan Kovachis, and Elle Truesdell. We had less than two months to pull it off- wanting to publish in October since baby is due in November. This dream team pulled together, and made it happen!

Molly- thank you for making me laugh over legless turkeys instead of crying. There is no one else I'd rather stuff my face with buffalo chicken dip with. You are so talented when it comes to styling all the dishes and capturing my cherished family recipes for this cookbook. Thank you for these beautiful pictures!

Morgan- thank you so much for leading the layout and design work for this book. All the hours that got poured into this book are very much appreciated. I thank you for making this book possible!

Elle- thank you so much for all the time you dedicated to transferring my handwritten and binder of recipes into this cookbook. Without all your support behind the scenes, we never could have done this!

To my Loves- the sweetest subscribers ever- without all of you, this book never would've happened. So many of you asked for this, and I truly believe God was speaking to me through you to make this cookbook. I am so glad you're here, and I can't wait to continue this journey with you! I am beyond grateful for our community.

GG- you are the best Gramma in the world. Thanks for always having patience with me, and letting me help you in the kitchen when I was little. Thank you for helping with the kids while I worked on this project, helping me to get all the recipes together, and for the time you dedicated to help me edit this book. I am so lucky to have you in my life, and I love you more than you could ever know.

Adam- thank you for fixing the stove when I was in crisis mode, midway through this book, and needing to bake tons of cookies. Thanks for always being supportive and encouraging me to follow my passions and the big dreams God puts on my heart. I love you!

Landon, Presley, and Little Babe- I love you so much my sweet babies! All the work I do is for you- you're the reason behind everything! Thank you for always helping me in the kitchen, and telling me how much you love my cooking. I hope you can use this cookbook with your families someday in the future, and remember how much love I will always have for you- more than every number, beyond infinity, I love you for forever!